Andrew Motion was born in 1952 and educated at University College, Oxford. His previous volumes of poetry are *The Pleasure Steamers* (1978), *Independence* (1981), *Secret Narratives* (1983), *Dangerous Play* (1986), and *Natural Causes* (1987). He has also published critical studies of Edward Thomas and Philip Larkin; a biography, *The Lamberts*; a novel, *The Pale Companion*; and edited with Blake Morrison *The Penguin Book of Contemporary British Poetry*. He is the authorized biographer of Philip Larkin. His work has been awarded the Arvon/*Observer* Poetry Prize, the John Llewelyn Rhys Prize, the Dylan Thomas Prize and the Somerset Maugham Prize. He lives in London with his wife and their three children.

Love in a Life   ANDREW MOTION

faber and faber

First published in 1991
by Faber and Faber Limited
3 Queen Square London WC1N 3AU

Photoset by Wilmaset, Birkenhead, Wirral
Printed in England by
Clays Ltd, St Ives plc

A CIP record for this book is available from the British Library

ISBN 0–571–16139–1
0–571–16101–4 (pbk)

For my children

Heart, fear nothing, for, heart, thou shalt find her –
Next time, herself! – not the trouble behind her
Left in the curtain, the couch's perfume!

Robert Browning, *Love in a Life*

Contents

PART ONE

Bad Dreams, 3
Look, 7
One Who Disappeared, 9
Judgement, 13
Cutting, 16
Run, 18
The Vision of that Ancient Man, 21
Cleaned Out, 24
Close, 26
A Blow to the Head, 28

PART TWO

The Prague Milk Bottle, 35
It is an Offence, 39
The Bone Elephant, 40

PART THREE

The Great Globe, 47
Toot Baldon, 48
Kanpur, 53
Belfast, 54
Hull, 57
Tamworth, 59

Acknowledgements

These poems in this book were first published by: *Harpers & Queen*; *Independent on Sunday*; *London Magazine*; *London Review of Books*; *Observer*; *Soho Square*; *Sunday Correspondent*; *Sunday Times*; *The Times*; *The Times Literary Supplement*.

PART ONE

Bad Dreams

1 DERBY TO ST PANCRAS

That sob through the wall
which bolts my heart
with its pure distress,
start-stops, and I'm left
in the prickly dark
with my eyes open wide
to a broken-off dream
still alive in my head.

Help me, Jannie,
lying beside me,
forget that I saw
last century's man
in a down train from Derby
(spats and port waistcoat
in clackety half-light),
whose hands were laced
round a bubble of glass
poised in his lap,
with the gift inside it
his sovereign had ordered –
the splayed purple hand
and puce second thumb
of the first and the only
bloom of a lily

to flower in the island
since time began.

Hold me, Jannie,
until I have seen him
through the last tunnels
and into St Pancras —
and not set him loose
to come back tomorrow,
and every tomorrow,
to show how the bloom
in its misty bubble
is dead as a stone,
how the beat of my heart
in time with his journey
is steadily slower,
and how as each morning
slops over the roof-tops
the sky's smear of red
is a sky weeping blood.

2 COLOMBIA ROAD

I happened just to be thinking
how twenty-one years ago
a girl I had barely met
lay with me day after day
(lay in my head, I mean)
on a white, unpeopled beach
or tucked in a crevice of wheat.

And I happened to say her name
aloud in Colombia Road
just as Jannie and I
were walking out one Sunday
past stall after stall of flowers:
Tulips? Carnations? Chrysanths?
Make up your mind! It's murder!

Jannie just happened to hear.
Bryony? Did you say Bryony?
I knew a Bryony once –
black eyes, her father farmed.
She died in a car, I think –
and there was a brother, or sister,
or both, or something or other . . .

Just then I happened to see
a dainty Victorian ship
sailing up to an island
somewhere near the equator,
drop anchor, and put down a boat
which wriggled into a bay
of silky turquoise water,

with someone crouched in the prow
who knew from others before him
that here and nowhere else
grew the most beautiful flower
ever to spring in the world,
of a colour to drive you mad
and scent to steal your heart,

and I happened to see him leap
smartly into the shallows
and scale a crumbling cliff
to find the island nothing
but glittering flakes of rock,
like a white unpeopled beach,
or a desert of dead grain.

Look

I pull back the curtain
and what do I see
but my wife on a sheet
and the screen beside her
showing our twins
out of their capsule
in mooning blue,
their dawdlers' legs
kicking through silence
enormously slowly,
while blotches beneath them
revolve like the earth
which will bring them to grief
or into their own.

I pull back the curtain
and what do I see
but my mother asleep,
or at least not awake,
and the sheet folded down
to show me her throat
with its wrinkled hole
and the tube inside
which leads to oxygen
stashed round her bed,
as though any day now
she might lift into space
and never return
to breathe our air.

I pull back the curtain
and what do I see
but the stars in the sky,
and their jittery light
stabbing through heaven
jabs me awake
from my dream that time
will last long enough
to let me die happy,
not yearning for more
like a man lost in space
might howl for the earth,
or a dog for the moon
with no reason at all.

One Who Disappeared

Did you ever hear me tell
of that woman whose only son
was walking the cliffs at Filey
a month after moving up here

(imagine them as strangers
new from the fug of the west,
and keen to snuff up air
blasting straight out of Russia)?

If you did, then you'll have heard
how he footed the tufty edge
like a drunk walking a line,
pompously,

proud to think himself sober,
and how the smothering thump
of waves bursting in caves
drowned his giggly shout

when he floated up in a paw
of wind ripping over the cliff
like stubble-fire through a hedge
and immediately dropped away

as if he was young Mr Punch
whipped from a bare stage
and falling a hundred feet
on sheets of black rock.

*

Our boy is ill,
When I loom above
his panting hush
he scalds my face.

I look and look
and he's always there
on his soaked pallet.
I look once more

and see the woman
who watches her son
for the millionth time
in his final second

snatching a handful
of splintery grass
from the chalk fringe
then leaving her

gaping,
clenching his fists
in the salt air
as hard on nothing

as I grip your hand
when you tiptoe in
and side by side
we gaze down

at our boy in silence,
like nervous spies
in an enemy country,
marooned on a beach

waiting for rescue,
scanning the sea
for the wink of a light
which is hours overdue.

*

I'm awake to a thrush
doodling with its voice,
to the scratchy fuss of sparrows,
to a blackbird chinking loose change,

and day swirls into the street
like milk billowed through tea –
a big light lightening nothing
as it colours the map of mountains

which is you beside me, sleeping,
that muzzy gap (the door),
and through it the luminous stripes
of the cot, lurching and snuffling.

Why do I feel that I've died
and am lingering here to haunt you?
Why don't I say your name?
Why don't I touch you?

I don't even feel I'm alive
when I hear the padded thwack
of the boy kicking round in his cot –
a soft crash, like the noise

of a splintered spar of wood
which falls in the night for no reason
a long way away in a builder's yard,
then is utterly still on the moonlit cement.

Judgement

I was raking leaves in the front bed
when a helicopter wittered overhead

and I saw a fish in a clear lake
when a waterbug paddles the far light.

My happiness disappeared. I had thought of death
and of everything that sails above the earth

brought low; I had watched the blood of my children
spill, and the hard stones at my feet crack open;

I had slithered so far into the underlying mud
I even flung out a hand for the hand of God.

*

Other times
I am underground:
when green minutes
drip from the clock
and wear me down
to the sort of bone
a scavenger dog
picks out of muck
and buries for later
but clean forgets,

so the years pass,
and the earth shifts,
and the bone turns
into nothing at all
like bone, or me,
or a single thing
waiting for light
and what it shows
of someone else
who lies awake
all night beside me
and never speaks.

*

For the first time in years
I am on my knees

in the sweet savour
of incense and soap.

The hand of God
is a burst of sunlight

torn through the head
of a window-saint;

the voice of God
is a fly in a web.

They are nothing to me.
I shut my eyes

and imagine a bed
overlooking a garden:

knee-high grass
and hysterical roses.

The day's almost done
and there's mist coming on.

An apple tree
by the farthest hedge

has the look of my wife
when her back is turned

and her head in her hands.
The best thing on earth

is to call her and ask
for a drink of water.

I call and call:
the kitchen tap;

a drink of water;
a drink of water

to taste and be sure
I am dying at home.

Cutting

In a break for the ads
I glimpsed the bar
where I used to be young.

A '30s detective
was quizzing a local
in clouds of tobacco:

flocks of pewter
flew up the wall;
a horse-brass winked;

and there on my tongue
was your darkest secret
like Old Virginia.

*

What became of the boy
who arrived on the dot

of visiting hour
and found that love

was wrecked in a fit?
Legs which were marble

snapped and high-stepped;
plaster-cast hands

panicked the sheets;
the head of a gorgon

had swallowed its tongue
but was begging to speak.

What became of the boy?
He was hurried away.

*

A hundred years old
at four in the morning,
we clamber and slide
like seals on the ice.
Where am I now?

A senseless hand
is squeezing my heart;
a broken cry
has called us together
and will not die.

Then the ice floes collapse
and here comes the sea.
I am dead to the world.
It is all as I thought.
And who might you be?

Run

In the small hours
I slipped back to childhood for a moment

and lay on my old bed with its view of the chestnut tree.
It was winter

and you had just died
so I was excited, still thinking your death was a thing apart

which soon I would put in the ground like a body
to visit from time to time, and otherwise forget.

*

But take Ruth
who drowned last week.

I used to fancy her –
now all I think
is what water can do,
easing off shoes,
making light
of the dense net of her tights.

To hell with out of place!
That's the fucking Thames dribbling down your face!

*

I dropped off
and dreamed I was in the Black Museum

where I met a woman six inches high,
hollow, white tunic, blue-green sash at the waist,

holding a basket of flames.
Her china face

had its features kissed away,
but the eyes were yours.

You could tell at a glance why some idiot thought
she was worth nothing at all.

*

Daylight breaks
and my children trawl
the drizzling passage
from their room to mine
which takes them years
but is only a step.

Sunk on the bed
of a parched lake
where sleep ran out,
I stare overhead
and brace myself
for their circle of eyes.

The time they arrive
is the time they go –
their almost inaudible
blobs of mouths
ooo-ing and aaah-ing
like shouting fish:

We travelled for ever
to reach your door,
and in the end
we found it locked.
Wake up, damn you!
Wish us good luck!

The Vision of that Ancient Man

I was taking a piss
when the dredger rode over our pleasure

like a swan rogering its mate
and we all sank down-a-down.

The porthole groaned and held . . .
the light went sick . . .

and eventually something shitty erupted out of the can
and I was a dead man.

    *

But I lived. Unlike my mate
I lived, and without her
I can't tell one thing from t'other.

First I went north to her house
where ever since everyone died
only a burglar had called –

a rock the size of a cat
crouched by the stinking hearth
in a bitter puddle of glass.

She never told me she lived
a stone's throw from the river!
At least I suppose the river

made that delectable voice
which kept me company there,
and not her copy of *Waverley*

gradually splitting its spine,
or her one dress which stayed
to rot in the dripping cupboard.

*

I lost everyone, everyone –
which makes me a murderer.
I must be a murderer, surely?
I know I wanted to die.

I came to a far countrie
the night of a hurricane
and hurled across the Channel
on a grainy bubble of spray.

The last thing I wanted to see
was myself at a breakfast table –
pink menus and waiters erect,
and outside, a sun-scattered sky!

*

There was someone else
before all this
who saw through life
and drowned herself.
Identify! Identify!

A family tie
and not the same
jerked inside out
on a shingle beach
in the morning light

as the one who wore
her best red dress
and matching smalls
the night before.
Identify! Identify!

She's in my life
like rock in a hill,
like leaves in a bud,
like heat in the sun,
like pips in a pear,

like . . . Sod it; who cares?

Cleaned Out

He was out for the day when a vanload of pricks
arrived at my father's house to steal his life:
the tables and chairs, the knick-knacks and pix,
the grandmother clock, all the family things.

*

I dream of falling
the centuries gone
like willow leaves
when storms roll up

the only life
a glacier stream
a samphire ledge
a fruiting tree.

*

I am your home, if you ever arrive;
I am dead; I am also alive.

I have lost my heart to the marsh
and my skin to ailing light and the wind's lash.

I am seeding grass in my muscular hands and feet;
I am fire and fleet.

I have carved my newfangled bones from a solid oak
no blaze, bereavement, battle or blow ever broke.

I am twigs in my fingers and hair;
I am curdled air.

Best of all is my voice from the springing south:
brilliant, particular leaves come rioting out of my mouth.

Close

The afternoon I was killed
I strolled up the beach from the sea
where the big wave had hit me,
helped my wife and kids
pack up their picnic things,
then took my place in the car
for the curving journey home
through almost-empty lanes.

I had never seen the country
looking so beautiful –
furnace red in the poppies
scribbled all over the fields;
a darker red in the rocks
which sheltered the famous caves;
and pink in the western sky
which bode us well for tomorrow.

Nobody spoke about me
or how I was no longer there.
It was odd, but I understood why:
when I had drowned I was only
a matter of yards out to sea
(not *too far out* – too close),
still able to hear the talk
and have everything safe in view.

My sunburned wife, I noticed,
was trying to change for a swim,
resting her weight on one leg
as if she might suddenly start
to dance, or jump in the air,
but in fact snaking out of her knickers –
as shy as she was undressing
the first time we went to bed.

A Blow to the Head

On the metro,
two stops in from Charles de Gaulle,
somebody slapped my wife.

Just like that –
a gang of kids –
for moving her bag
from the seat to her lap:
a thunderclap
behind my back.

Very next thing
was reeling dark
and the kids outside
beside themselves:
You didn't see! You didn't see!
It might be him! It wasn't me!

For the rest,
she wept through every station into Paris,
her head on my shoulder like love at the start of its life.

*

By the merest chance
I had in mind
J. K. Stephen,
who damaged his head
on a visit to Felix-
stowe (Suffolk) in '86.

The nature of the accident is not certainly known;
in the Stephen family it was said he was struck
by some projection from a moving train.

Not a serious blow,
but it drove him mad
(molesting bread
with the point of a sword;
seized with genius –
painting all night),

and finally killed him
as well as his father,
who two years later
surrendered his heart
with a definite crack
like a sla . . .

    *

. . . which reminds me.
When I was a kid
a man called Morris
slapped my face
so crazily hard
it opened a room
inside my head
where plates of light
skittered and slid
and wouldn't quite
fit, as they were
meant to, together.

It felt like the way,
when you stand between mirrors,
the slab of your face
shoots backwards and forwards
for ever and ever
with tiny delays,
so if you could only
keep everything still
and look to the end
of the sad succession,
time would run out
and you'd see yourself dead.

          *

There is an attic flat
with views of lead
where moonlight rubs
its greasy cream,

and a serious bed
where my darling wife
lies down at last
and curls asleep.

I fit myself
along her spine
but dare not touch
her breaking skull,

and find my mother
returns to me
as if she was climbing
out of a well:

ginger with bruises,
hair shaved off,
her spongy crown
is ripe with blood.

I cover my face
and remember a dog
in a reeking yard
when the kid I was

came up to talk.
I was holding a choc
in a folded fist,
but the dog couldn't tell

and twitched away –
its snivelling whine
like human fear,
its threadbare head

too crankily sunk
to meet my eye
or see what I meant
by my opening hand.

PART TWO

The Prague Milk Bottle

for Ivo Smoldas

The astrological clock
produces its twelve apostles
every hour

in a brainless, jerking parade
as windows wheeze open and shut,
Death twitches,

bells ping, and the cockerel crows
like a model train at a crossing
while I

get drunk in the sunlit square with Ivo
surrounded by skirts as if nothing is wrong
except:

my bathplug won't fill the hole,
my water is cold,
my phone-call to home never works,
the exchange rate is shit,

and the milk!

— the milk of kindness, our mother's milk,
comes in a thing of French design,
looks like a condom and leaks like a sieve
and keeps us screaming most of the time.

*

In your wildest dreams you might whistle
and two ravens would flit their dark forest
for a baroque room you know is the British Embassy
(it has a view of Prague unmatched except by the Palace).

The ravens turn into girls and are painfully beautiful,
leaning with bare arms entwined,
black dresses crushed to the back of a yellow sofa
to take in the city you never expected to see from this angle:

miraculous spires; ecstatic saints shattered by God;
and cobbled streets where the girls will squirm in your palm
then fold into wings and fly off with a gasp –
the sound of you waking alone in your dark hotel.

*

It's not suppression,
it's humiliation.

The men they put in power
(they aren't stupid) – some of them
can hardly speak a sentence.

It's not suppression,
it's humiliation.

I have a headache. Nothing much,
but threatening to be worse – a tension
like the silence in a clock before it strikes.

It's not suppression,
it's humiliation.

My chemist writes prescriptions
but we have no drugs. I wish him ill.
None of this has much to do with girls.

It's not suppression,
it's humiliation.

*

I leave Ivo to himself
and two hours later
he's outside the airport
hoisting a bag
of toys for my children.

It's like seeing the ghost
of a friend whose death
made you say everything
there was to say.
Now there is nothing.

The milk of kindness
floods our eyes,
or perhaps it's grit
swirled on the tarmac
in tottering cones.

We nod good-bye
where Security starts
and men in gloves
count my balls,
then I slither away

down a dingy tunnel
and turn again
to Ivo pinned
on a block of light
the size of a stamp,

his mechanical arm
glumly aloft,
his mouth ajar
to show he is screaming
if I could just hear.

Spring 1989

It is an Offence

The man in the flats opposite keeps a whippet
(once a racer) and two or three times a week
it craps by my front door – sloped, weary turds
like a single file of slugs in battle fatigues
(surprisingly slow for a whippet) – so that often
my shoes, my wife's, our children's bring it back home
to the stairs, the skirting, the carpets, the kitchen tiles
in bobbles or flakes or hanks or outrageous slithery smears.

The sad old dog doesn't know what he's doing, and yet
I'd still like to cover his arsehole with quick-set cement.

I admit that I also yearn to leave my mark on society,
and not see machines or people trample it foolishly.

On the one hand it's only shit; on the other, shit's shit,
and what we desire in the world is less, not more, of it.

The Bone Elephant

Like a toy in a box
my father's tank
crouched in the hold
of a flat-bottomed boat,
its toady green
lit with spray,
and my father inside
a leaden soldier
thrown into fire.

Then the Channel was blocked
but still too deep,
so the first tank off
stalled and sank –
which meant my father
reached dry land
by crushing the head
of a man who drowned
and was also his friend.

Bars of mud
in my father's tracks
from Essex and Kent
and Wiltshire and York
were spurted away
when he hit the beach
and the country ahead
became his home
and all he knew:

the metal orchards
erupting in blossom,
ponds in secret
corners of pasture,
the road he cast
over towns and woods
like a floating line
which was heavy as lead
and smashed them apart.

*

In a snicket off Wenceslas Square
I was thinking of buying a hat.

'A hat? It's not very green –
it is fox – a Muscovite hat:

admire it here, in the silver,
and here, in the bronze.

We are used to talking in circles
(my generation, my father's) –

We cannot take a straight line
or rise on each other's shoulders.

Try it and see! How is that?
The band, I think, is too tight –

you can't run your finger round here,
as if wiping your brow, so *bang* –

a migraine will come. We have no others,
I'm sorry. Yes thank you, sterling is fine.'

*

I left home for good
and took from my father
a miniature elephant,
smooth and hard
as the joint of a saint,

which had jolted through France
in his battledress pocket,
then fallen down drunk
and snapped one leg
when peace descended.

It lives on the plain
of my mantelpiece,
up to its ears
in postcards and junk,
with one eye fixed

on the way to escape,
and one eye on me
as I drink up the news
from a misty TV:
a tank is surfing

an ocean of faces;
someone has reached
the heart of Berlin
and thrown his hat
a mile in the air;

there's someone else rising
on everyone's shoulders,
hugging the sky
which roars his name
close to his chest,

then spreading his arms
above Wenceslas Square
like a fisherman showing
the largest fish
his heart could desire.

Winter 1989

PART THREE

The Great Globe

The border was neither wide nor deep, but it took a day
to sieve it, working through sprays of gravel, London clay,
and the bonfire wrecks left by people before us:
sheets of sick iron, charred bottles, batteries leaking pus.

I thought of Joanna; the brittle white china body
I smashed, she smashed and hid, but which still cuts me
out of the deep solid earth wrestling and fretting like the sea.

Toot Baldon

You were Caesar's wife before you were mine
and that's how I saw you first: a sleek hawk
borne in on a tremor of light when the curtain rose
and dangling in heavy shadow behind the throne.

Now that you're somebody's wife again,
your naked wings, your white contemptuous face
are triggered by anything under the sun:
my short-cut to work, for instance,

which means I slip past the Dominion each day
and see, by the door where the stars come out,
tracks of stilettos pricked into tarmac –
claw-marks in snow, after the birds have flown.

    *

When first we were married
and I was Edward Thomas,
and you were no more Helen
than bloody Marie of Romania,

we rented an attic flat
like a boat (hunched ceilings
and lop-sided walls)
on course for open country.

Our view from the sitting-room bow
was a green drop through sky
and a crinkled wave of elms
to fields where a herd of Friesians

drifted like cumulus shadows –
fields dotted and dashed with nettle,
dreamily rolling and lifting
as if they were canvas flapped out

and billowing up to the Chilterns.
That was the plan of our walk –
Adam and Eve in love
on a wandering contour of mud

which swerved down a tunnel of beech
and came out at last on the hills.
It was there that our choices began:
on to the clouds, then home?

I've forgotten the ways we went,
but never that trampled patch
where the path split up like veins
wriggling away from a heart

and we would decide to go forwards,
or sideways, or back,
and maybe lean for a breath
on a mangled crab-apple stump

collapsed years before,
or gingerly stoop and peer
over the tottering walls
of a pen someone had built

which never held hide nor hair
of any creature we'd seen,
though one we supposed had littered there,
then been drummed back to her yard.

*

It might be happening now
when I see us kneel at the kerb
in a dry stream of grit.

We are past the witching hour
and this is Longwall Street:
not a sound from Magdalen's trees,

no late night walkers' voices
drowning the faint click-blink
of traffic-lights marking time

although no traffic draws up.
It's like the still seconds to come
just after a droning siren

has driven the world to hide,
and the air goes deaf with screaming.
But the seconds pass and it's not

screams I hear but a sigh.
I am cradling the head of a girl
we've come across – simple as that –

trounced into rags in the gutter,
her bike like a broken puzzle
flung down in the swerving road.

On my hand, on the hard tarmac,
blood is slipping – not much,
but more than enough to explain

the way her eyes keep glaring
angrily into mine
as if I was all she loved,

and why they lose their light
like stones picked out of water
and left to dry in the sun.

Then the police appear
and carefully shoosh us away –
arms out as though we were sheep

to be squeezed through a narrow gate –
and we're back in the darkened home
we are trying to make together,

undressing for bed like strangers
who haven't a clue what to say,
but already imagine a morning

when they will awake alone,
with sunlight splitting the curtains
to pour its fatuous heat

in the vacant space beside them:
the perfect undimpled pillow;
the blank sheet.

Kanpur

That light-sleeping night
slip-slap, slip-slap
was surely a servant
about his own business
in black marble halls.

Or was it the Ganges
compiling its sandbanks
just under our window
then sloshing them flat
to a gluey green ripple?

No. It was the smack
of wet white plaster
dropped from the roof
on our separate beds
and the space between us,

which showed next day
the dandering footprints
a lizard had scrawled
as it passed us by
without our knowledge.

Belfast

I've been over to root up my man
but the ground is hard as a stone.

His houses are both torn down.

His woman has moved.

His writing paper is dust
lining a mouse's nest.

And the marvellous records which made him cry
are smashed and buried miles out of town
in that dump you pass on the airport road
where everyone's rubbish goes when they die.

        *

When I last flew away
I was home in time
to find you out.

You had taken your man
along the canal
where no one would see.

But I saw at once:
each eager hair
on his lanky head,

his yellow smile
which flicked like a fish
in stagnant reaches.

Yes, I saw it all
just from the way
your knives and forks

lay criss-crossed
on the draining-board
in a crackling silence.

*

That was another life –
but even in this one,
this new happy one,
it has taken less than a week
in a blank, stripped-pine hotel
to be lonely as hell.

On the wet road below
a grey Land-Rover-woodlouse
gets a wide bearth, and gives
a wild glimpse of soldiers
hunched behind toughened glass.
I was forgetting where I was!

*

My taxi for Aldegrove
is cooling outside the bar
while the driver makes time
for talk and a quick jar:

Haven't found much out, then?
I dare say not.
At this late stage in history
the past is one flat field of shit.

It's no good. No matter how
desperately your man A loves your B
they forget them, or start
lying about them eventually.

You don't mind plain-speaking
do you? You do? Right; let's go.
What with it being Guy Fawkes and all
there'll be dire delays on the road.

Hull

This is the park where Larkin lived
– moss-haired statues and dusty grass! –
and a year or so after he'd packed and gone
        you lived here too

in one of those gaunt Victorian flats
where heat flies up to the ceiling and clings
in the intricate mesh of its moulding, leaving you
        frozen

whatever the weather, although it was freezing
in fact the day that I tried to persuade you
our life could go on, and we grappled for nearly
        an hour

on your hideous sofa (its bristling cloth
like tonsured hair which cannot grow back),
gasping and gritting our teeth and finally just
        giving up

whereupon you plunged into your jersey again
and picked up a book, while I – pretending
nothing unusual had happened – went to the window
        and saw

a man in a belted mac returning from work
– a respectable man: brown glasses and trilby hat –
stop under one of the cavernous chestnuts,
        fling

his briefcase heavily into the branches,
crouch in a hail of conkers, chase them
hither and yon in the cobwebby shade,
            pocket them,

then disappear in the gloaming along with the others
you learn to expect in a shat-upon dump like this:
home-going clerks, litter-bin-lunatics, drunks,
            and those

who stand at their darkening windows and think
if they hurry there's time to get dressed and go out
and begin the day over again – with a visit, perhaps,
            to the plant-house

which glistens below, full of strangers who flounder
aimlessly round and round in its tropical bubble,
nod to each other through floppy-tongued leaves,
            and once in a while

stop at the cage where a moth-eaten minah bird
squats on its metal bough and says nothing at all
except – if you scare him badly enough –
            his name.

Tamworth

Red brick on red brick.

A boiled eye in a greenhouse.

Lilac smoking in sere gutters and crevices.

A pigtailed head on lamp-post after lamp-post.

*

We had taken my mother's estate
and driven into the blue –
she was in hospital then,
and didn't care.

*

Out of nowhere, nowhere else to go,
stuck in the dead afternoon, collapsed,

the mushroom hush of the lounge bar oozing up
through bilious carpet into our bed,

while men in the country nearby poked long rods
in voluptuous hedgerows, streams, rush-clumps,

fidgeting over the cracked hillsides shouting
Nothing here!, flinching at shadows, cursing.

*

We'd zigzagged over the map
seeing cathedral cities —
any excuse had done
to get us a week alone.

That evening under Southwell's
swarthy prolific leaves
an imp in a fissure of oak
might have been Robin Hood.

    *

It was not for us. It was death —
though the men came back empty-handed,
grinning, and stacked their long poles in the yard.

They understood when we packed and paid.
There were other towns, sure — plenty,
if we could hurry — our last hour of day

squeezed by a storm fuming from Nottingham way:
pitch, lemon-yellow, beech-green,
champing till ready, flighting a few big blobs

as the dusty country we entered
braced and opened itself — leaf-hands splayed and grasping,
toads pushing up stones, mercury ponds blinking.

    *

We'd kitted out the car
with a mattress in the back,
and a sort of gyppo curtain
exactly for nights like this.

Before we left the outskirts
we posted my mother a card,
knowing my father would read it
stooping above her bed:

Fantastic carving at Southwell!
The car's going a bomb!
Not one puncture yet!
The back's really comfy!

*

The thing we did – the thing anyone like us did –
was find ourselves lost and be glad of it,
chittering to and fro in a lane-labyrinth
with its centre a stubble bank at the head of a valley.

Therefore we went no further. Therefore we simply sat
and watched the sky perform: elephant clouds at first
with their distant wobble and bulge like ink underwater,
then splits of thunder, then the sour flash of light

glancing off metal, then clouds with their hair slicked back,
edgy, crouching to sprint, and when sprinting at last
fanned flat, guttering, flicking out ochre tongues
before losing their heads altogether, boiled down

to a Spanish skirt cartwheeling through woods,
a heavy boot squelching out squall after squall
of brickdust, nail, hair, and Christ knows what
shrieks and implorings we never caught even a word of.

*

We burrowed against each other
after the storm had gone,
and saw between our curtains
lightning over the valley

on its nimble silver legs –
one minute round our car,
the next high up in heaven
kicking splinters off stars –

then skipping away to somewhere
with the thunder-dog behind it
grumbling but exhausted,
and leaving us such silence

I'd swear I heard the moon
creak as it entered the sky,
and the stubble field around us
breathing earth-smell through its bristles.